Gnarly Skateboarders

X-MOVES

by **Michael Sandler**

Consultant: Steve Cave
Skateboarding Expert
www.skateboard.about.com

BEARPORT
PUBLISHING

New York, New York

Credits

Cover and Title Page, © Matt Stroshane/Getty Images; TOC, © Guillermo Trejos/iStockphoto 4, © Bo Bridges/Corbis; 5, © AP Images/Reed Saxon; 6, © Grant Brittain; 7, © Bill Eppridge//Time Life Pictures/Getty Images; 8, © Glen E. Friedman; 9, © Glen E. Friedman; 10, © AP Images/Chris Carlson; 11, © Stefan Zeig; 12L, © Christian Petersen/Getty Images; 12R, © Carl Schneider/Ultimate Group, LLC/Alamy; 13, © Tony Donaldson/Icon SMI; 14, © AP Images/Mark J. Terrill; 15, © Matt Stroshane/Getty Images; 16, © Cameron Spencer/Getty Images; 17, © Rodrigo Paiva/Reuters/Landov; 18, Courtesy of Mike Blabac/DC Shoes; 19T, © AP Images/Greg Baker; 19B, © Mike Blabac/UPI Photo/Landov; 20, Courtesy of Jamie Mosberg/Digital Action Sports Network/BobBurnquist.com; 21, © Courtesy of Jamie Mosberg/Digital Action Sports Network/BobBurnquist.com; 22, © Tomasz Trojanowski/Shutterstock.

Publisher: Kenn Goin
Senior Editor: Lisa Wiseman
Creative Director: Spencer Brinker
Photo Researcher: James O'Connor

Helmets are a skateboarder's most important piece of safety gear. If you try skateboarding, wear one. It's the only way to skate.

Library of Congress Cataloging-in-Publication Data

Sandler, Michael, 1965-
  Gnarly skateboarders / by Michael Sandler.
    p. cm. — (X-moves)
  Includes bibliographical references and index.
  ISBN-13: 978-1-59716-950-9 (library binding)
  ISBN-10: 1-59716-950-1 (library binding)
1. Skateboarding—Juvenile literature. I. Title.

  GV859.8.S26 2010
  796.22—dc22
                              2009002156

For more information, write to Bearport Publishing Company, Inc., 101 Fifth Avenue, Suite 6R, New York, New York 10003. Printed in the United States of America.

10 9 8 7 6 5 4 3 2 1

Contents

Flying and Falling

Skateboarder Jake Brown rocketed down the 300-foot-long (91-m) Mega Ramp. He soared across a 70-foot (21-m) **gap** and launched his best trick. He was trying to complete a double spin called a **720**. It was the first time anyone had tried to do the **stunt** in **Big Air** history.

Jake landed it! Then he sped up the **quarterpipe** to the finish. Suddenly, the skateboard flew one way and Jake flew another. He fell 45 feet (14 m)—almost five stories—to the ground.

Jake lay motionless, crumpled in a heap. Then, amazingly, he was able to get up and walk. Jake was then rushed to the hospital. He was lucky to have survived.

Jake soars off the Mega Ramp.

Jake losing his board before falling hard during the Big Air competition

When Jake fell, he was competing in the Big Air competition at **X Games** 13 in Los Angeles, California, in 2007. This event gives skateboarders nightmares. Why? The Mega Ramp is so high that skaters need to use an elevator to reach the starting point.

From Surfing to Skating

Skateboarders like Jake Brown didn't always fly through the air. Instead, the first skateboarders glided across flat California sidewalks. The sport was invented in the 1950s by bored **surfers**. They wanted something to do on days when the ocean was too calm for surfing.

To make the skateboards, surfers stuck roller-skate wheels onto wooden boards and rolled down the street. The surfers couldn't do many tricks. The boards were too slow and heavy.

As time passed, however, the boards got lighter and faster. Soon, skaters were flying up ramps, popping wheelies, and doing handstands.

An early skateboard

LIFE

The craze and
the menace of

SKATEBOARDS

San Diego's Pat McGee,
national girls' champion,
does a handstand on wheels

MAY 14 · 1965 · 35¢

Lighter, faster skateboards were made using wood combined with **fiberglass**. Along with **kicktails** and better wheels, these boards allowed skaters to start doing more tricks.

National girl's champion Pat McGee did a handstand on a skateboard for the cover of *Life* magazine on May 14, 1965.

Vert Skating

In the 1970s, riders looked for new places to skate. Concrete pipes, drainage ditches, and empty swimming pools challenged them to create new tricks.

In pools, skateboarders rode up the smooth sides. They did **grinds**, dragging their **trucks** across the pool's edge. They poked their boards above the pool's **lip**. Some popped all four wheels over. Now the skaters were flying. They called this trick catching **air**.

These new tricks were the beginning of **vertical**, or vert, skating. This meant that the boards weren't level with the ground. They were pointed toward the sky.

Stacy Peralta, shown here, was part of a group of skaters from Santa Monica, California, called the Z-Boys. They were vert **pioneers**.

Tony Alva, shown here, was also one of the Z-Boys. In 1977, he became famous for doing the first official air in skateboarding history.

Street Skating

In the 1980s, a different style of skating began to reach new levels—street skating. Skaters started to look at curbs, flower planters, and benches in a whole new way. These everyday objects weren't **obstacles**: they were opportunities. Street skaters used them to put a new spin on tricks like grinds and **boardslides**. They glided down stairway handrails. They hopped from sidewalks to benches and back again

The ollie was the key first trick for street skaters to master. It got you off the ground. Once you were there, you could do almost anything.

A skateboarder slides down the handrail of a building in California.

The ollie

1 The skater slams the board's tail down against the ground.

2 The skater jumps upward.

3 The skater levels the board.

4 The skater lands back on the ground.

Florida skateboarder Alan "Ollie" Gelfand invented the ollie in 1977. He was just 13 years old.

Competitions

At skateboard competitions, skaters test both vert skills and street skills. In vert events, skateboarders make runs on **halfpipes** that vary in size. Judges score their tricks for style, **consistency**, and difficulty. Amplitude, which means how high they sail into the air, is also part of the score.

In street events, skaters ride courses filled with obstacles—ramps, rails, and boxes. Judges score them on the number of tricks they perform in a given amount of time. Difficulty and **originality** count, too.

At the X Games, which usually feature Vert, Street, and Big Air competitions, men and women compete in separate events. Karen Jones won the gold for Women's Vert at X Games 14 in 2008.

Karen Jones competing during the Women's Vert event at X Games 14 in 2008

A halfpipe

Ryan Sheckler won the Street Skateboarding gold at X Games 14.

Best Tricks

In addition to vert and street, some competitions also have a best trick event. In best trick, skaters pull out their toughest moves, their very best stunts. Sometimes they perform tricks that have never been done before. Tony Hawk did just that at X Games 5 on June 27, 1999. He landed the world's first ever 900.

What is a 900? It's an air trick in which the skater spins two and a half times before landing. It's enough to make a person dizzy.

Champion skater Lyn-Z Adams Hawkins always has the best tricks.

Tony Hawk, shown here, failed to complete the 900 on his first 10 attempts. He landed it on his 11th try.

Ten years after Tony's 900 at X Games 5, only a few other people in the world have ever landed the trick. No one, however, has landed a 1080—three full spins—though Shaun White tried at the 2006 X Games.

Around the World

America's X Games isn't the only big skateboard competition. Contests take place all over the world—from Mexico to Japan. World Cup Skateboarding (WCS) holds events on three continents. The rider with the best overall score in these tournaments is the champion.

The AST Dew Tour in the United States is one of the biggest WCS skating contests after the X Games. Another competition, Brazil's Rio Skate Jam, is where legendary skater Bob Burnquist has shown off many of his best tricks. People think skateboarding will be added to the Olympics in 2012 or 2016.

A skater competes at the Bondi Beach Bowl-A-Rama annual skate competition, a WCS event, in Australia.

Bob Burnquist

Bob Burnquist grew up in São Paulo, Brazil. He began skating at the age of 11. Today, he's considered to be one of the best vert skaters in the world.

17

Daredevil Tricks

Some skateboard tricks are just too extreme for competitions, so they are performed in other places. Many are the work of San Diego skater Danny Way. In 1997, Danny took air to a whole new level. He called his trick the "Bomb Drop." He jumped out of a helicopter to land safely on a ramp.

Over the years, Danny has set record after record—for the highest airs and longest distances jumped. His most famous **feat** came in 2005. Danny became the first person in history to leap by skateboard over the Great Wall of China.

Danny Way jumps out of a helicopter while performing the Bomb Drop.

Danny Way jumps the Great Wall of China.

Danny isn't just famous for his tricks. He's also the inventor of the Mega Ramp used in the X Games' Big Air event.

No Limits

There are few limits to skateboarding's extreme tricks. Street skaters are always finding new ways to slide and grind. Vert skaters add more **rotations** to their spins. Big Air skaters push the limits despite the dangers.

Jake Brown was knocked unconscious after falling from the Mega Ramp at X Games 13. When he woke up, he wanted to know only one thing: "Did I make the 720?"

For daredevil skaters, the biggest problem is finding new places to jump from. After all, who can top Bob Burnquist's 2006 trick? He skated down a 40-foot (12-m) ramp, up a 40-foot (12-m) rail, and into the Grand Canyon. Now that's big air!

The ramp that Bob Burnquist skated down at the Grand Canyon

Bob, after skating down the ramp, swooped up a rail before sailing into the air over the Grand Canyon.

Bob Burnquist fell 1,600 feet (488 m) into the Grand Canyon. How did he survive? Bob opened a parachute after speeding off the rail.

Skateboarding 101

To skate down the biggest ramps and perform the toughest tricks, skateboarders need special equipment.

Helmet
Keeps your head safe; always wear one for protection

Wrist and Elbow Pads
Protect your wrists and elbows during a crash

Deck
The top where you stand

Nose
The front of a skateboard

Knee Pads
Protect your knees during a crash

Skate Shoes
Tough and grippy so your feet don't slide off the board during tricks

Trucks
Connect the wheels to the board

Urethane Wheels
Smooth wheels for easy rolling

Kicktail
The back end of a skateboard; press down and the nose goes up in the air

Glossary

air (AIR) a trick in which a skateboarder rides into the air

Big Air (BIG AIR) a skateboarding event held on a Mega Ramp

boardslides (BORD-slidez) tricks in which a person slides along an object with the board's underside—not the wheels—making contact with the object

consistency (kuhn-SIS-tuhnt-see) doing something over and over with the same level of quality each time

feat (FEET) an act or achievement that takes courage, skill, or strength

fiberglass (FYE-bur-*glass*) a strong material made from very fine threads of glass

gap (GAP) a space between two things

grinds (GRYNDZ) tricks done by grinding a skateboard's truck against the rail or lip of a ramp

halfpipes (HAF-pipes) U-shaped ramps used for vert skating tricks

kicktails (KIK-taylz) the back ends of skateboards

lip (LIP) the upper edge of a swimming pool or ramp

obstacles (OB-stuh-kuhlz) things that block a path

originality (uh-*rij*-uh-NAL-i-tee) something that hasn't been done before

pioneers (*pye*-uh-NEERZ) the first people to do something

quarterpipe (KWOR-tur-*pipe*) a curved ramp that is one half of a halfpipe

rotations (roh-TAY-shuhnz) full spins

720 (*sev*-in-TWEN-tee) a trick in which the skateboarder makes two complete spins in the air

stunt (STUHNT) a trick or dangerous act that takes skill and bravery to perform

surfers (SURF-urz) people who use long boards to ride on ocean waves

trucks (TRUHKS) the metal hardware that the wheels of skateboards are attached to

vertical (VUR-tuh-kuhl) in an up-and-down direction

X Games (EKS GAYMZ) an extreme sports competition held every year

Bibliography

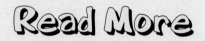

Brisick, Jamie. *Have Board Will Travel: The Definitive History of Surf, Skate, and Snow.* New York: HarperCollins (2004).

Davis, James. *Skateboarding Is Not a Crime: 50 Years of Street Culture.* Buffalo, NY: Firefly (2004).

Weyland, Jocko. *The Answer Is Never: A Skateboarder's History of the World.* New York: Grove Press (2002).

Read More

Abraham, Philip. *Extreme Sports Stars.* New York: Scholastic (2007).

Anderson, Jameson. *The Z-Boys and Skateboarding.* Mankato, MN: Capstone (2007).

Streissguth, Thomas. *Skateboarding Street Style.* Minneapolis, MN: Bellwether (2008).

Learn More Online

To learn more about skateboarding's tricks, stars, and competitions, visit
www.bearportpublishing.com/X-Moves

Index